# Dear Parent:

Congratulations! Your child is taking the first steps on an exciting journey. The destination? Independent reading!

**STEP INTO READING**® will help your child get there. The program offers five steps to reading success. Each step includes fun stories and colorful art. There are also Step into Reading Sticker Books, Step into Reading Math Readers, Step into Reading Phonics Readers, Step into Reading Write-In Readers, and Step into Reading Phonics Boxed Sets—a complete literacy program with something to interest every child.

## Learning to Read, Step by Step!

**Ready to Read   Preschool–Kindergarten**
• big type and easy words • rhyme and rhythm • picture clues
For children who know the alphabet and are eager to begin reading.

**Reading with Help   Preschool–Grade 1**
• basic vocabulary • short sentences • simple stories
For children who recognize familiar words and sound out new words with help.

**Reading on Your Own   Grades 1–3**
• engaging characters • easy-to-follow plots • popular topics
For children who are ready to read on their own.

**Reading Paragraphs   Grades 2–3**
• challenging vocabulary • short paragraphs • exciting stories
For newly independent readers who read simple sentences with confidence.

**Ready for Chapters   Grades 2–4**
• chapters • longer paragraphs • full-color art
For children who want to take the plunge into chapter books but still like colorful pictures.

**STEP INTO READING**® is designed to give every child a successful reading experience. The grade levels are only guides. Children can progress through the steps at their own speed, developing confidence in their reading, no matter what their grade.

Remember, a lifetime love of reading starts with a single step!

To Jeff Fine, who understands the beauty and
mystery of train tracks
—S.E.G.

To Brooks
—M.J.D.

**Acknowledgments:** Thanks to designers Francisco Lupin and Priestmangoode for their incredible designs for future trains, Chris Whitten of Interesting.com for the old-time train illustration, Ghislain Gerard for access to his extensive archive of train pictures, the Canadian Pacific Railway for its excellent photo archive, and Jennifer Jo and the Ringling Bros. and Barnum & Bailey Circus. And, finally, thanks to Georgia for putting up with having her picture taken so many times in a small sleeping car, coming home from Chicago.

**Photograph and illustration credits:** Cover: © Jan L. Kaulins; pp. 1, 41: © Dreamstime; p. 3: © Matthew Black/Wikipedia; p. 4: © Chris Laurens/Alamy; p. 6: © Arch White/Alamy; p. 7: John Paul Photography; p. 9: © Photolibrary/All Canada Photos; p. 12: © National Railway Museum/ Science & Society Picture Library; p. 13: courtesy of Interesting.com; p. 14: © Mar Photographics/ Alamy; pp. 15, 18 (bottom): © Corbis; pp. 16–17: derivative work from original licensed GFDL Cc-by-sa-2.5, 2.0, 1.0/Wikipedia; p. 18 (top): © Union Pacific Railroad Museum; p. 19: © Library of Congress; p. 20: © Science & Society Picture Library/Getty; pp. 21, 24, 25, 29, 31: © Ghislain Gerard; pp. 22–23, 39, 43: Photolibrary; pp. 26, 28: courtesy Canadian Pacific Railway; p. 27: Keith Desbois/U.S. Army; p. 30: Heinz Kluetmeier © 2010 Feld Entertainment; p. 34: © Chad Ehlers/ Alamy; p. 36: © Greg O'Beirne/Wikipedia; p. 37: © Saul Loeb/Getty; p. 38: © Shyali/Dreamstime; p. 40: © Bloomberg/Getty; p. 42: © Peter Bowater/Alamy; pp. 44–45, 47: © Priestmangoode; p. 46: © Francisco Lupin; p. 48: © Artaniss8/Dreamstime.

Visit us on the Web!
StepIntoReading.com
www.randomhouse.com/kids

Educators and librarians, for a variety of teaching tools, visit us at
www.randomhouse.com/teachers

*Library of Congress Cataloging-in-Publication Data*
Goodman, Susan E.
Trains! / by Susan E. Goodman; photographs taken and selected by Michael J. Doolittle.
   p. cm.
ISBN 978-0-375-86941-9 (trade) — ISBN 978-0-375-96941-6 (lib. bdg.) —
ISBN 978-0-375-98345-0 (ebook)
1. Railroad trains—Juvenile literature. I. Doolittle, Michael J. II. Title.
TF148.G66 2012   625.2—dc22   2011002910

Printed in the United States of America    10 9 8 7 6 5 4 3 2 1

# Trains!

By Susan E. Goodman
Photographs taken and selected
by Michael J. Doolittle

Random House 🏠 New York

# All Aboard!

Hop on a train.

They are a great way to travel.

New ones fly down the tracks.

Old trains are fun too.

They click-clack on old tracks.

They let you pretend

you are living long ago.

New or old,

trains are an adventure.

This train's name is the Jacobite.

Mostly it takes people

home or to work.

It passes lakes.

It crosses bridges.

Other times, it's a movie star!

It plays the Hogwarts Express.

It takes Harry Potter

and his friends to school.

What's the best thing
about a train ride?
Sometimes it's what you see
outside your window.

This trip has great scenery.

Sadly, there are no passengers

to see it.

The train is coming from a mine.

It is carrying salt to a factory.

But the crew can enjoy the view!

The best thing about a trip

may be the train itself.

Trains can be hotels in motion!

You can rent your own room.

It is very small.

But you have everything you need.

You can read.

You can wash up.

You can get a good night's sleep!

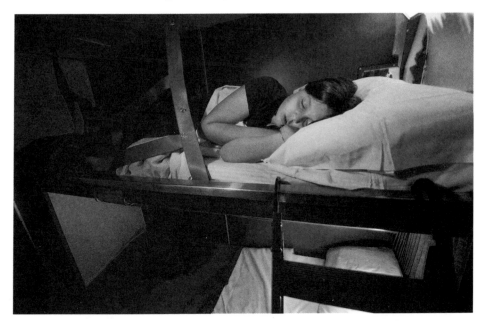

The restaurant car

serves meals all day long!

Trains are an adventure.

# The Age of the Railroad

In 1829

George Stephenson built

the first modern locomotive.

He called it the Rocket.

It raced about 35 miles an hour!

Its speed changed the world.
Stagecoaches took four days
to travel 150 miles.
Trains took only four hours.
The Age of the Railroad began.
Soon trains were running
all over the world.

Early trains ran on steam power.

Engines burned coal

to boil water.

The water turned to steam.

The steam built up

and pushed parts of the engine.

These parts moved

and turned the wheels.

# Here are the parts of a steam train:

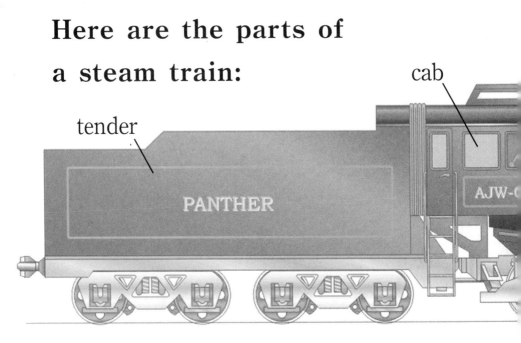

tender

cab

PANTHER

AJW-

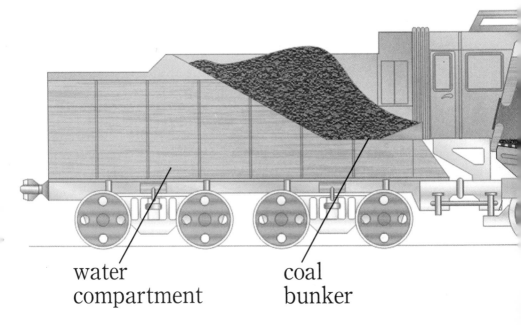

water
compartment

coal
bunker

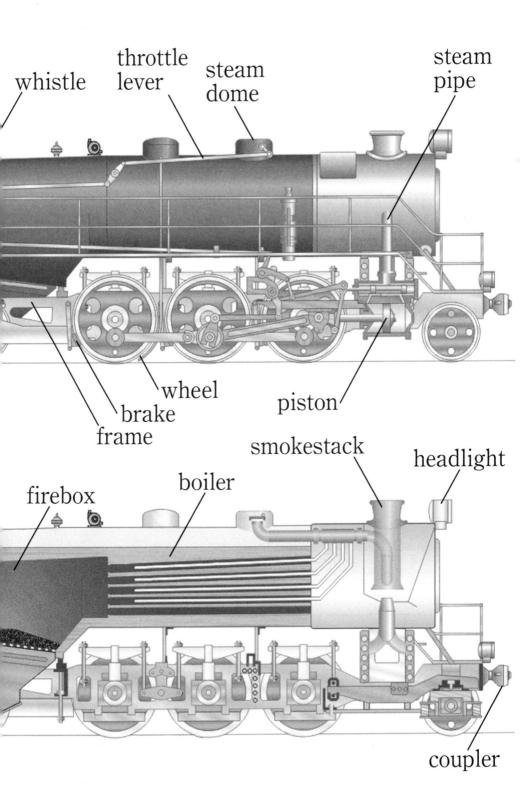

whistle

throttle lever

steam dome

steam pipe

wheel

brake

frame

piston

smokestack

headlight

firebox

boiler

coupler

By 1860 the eastern United States

had many railroads.

But the country needed one

to go from coast to coast.

In 1863 work began in the West.

Workers built bridges over rivers.

They blasted through mountains.

In 1869 two engines

faced each other in Utah.

One had traveled from the East.

The other came from the West.

One last rail

would connect all the tracks.

Workers hammered it in

with a spike of solid gold!

Trains carried cargo and people.

Some even carried queens!

Queen Victoria of England

had her own train.

It was the first one to have

a bathroom in it!

Trains used steam power
for a long time.
Then the diesel engine took over.
It burns oil to make electricity.
The electricity drives the train.
Diesels are cheaper to run
than steam engines.
They do not need as much repair.
We still use diesel engines today.

# Pulling Weight,
# Pulling Freight

Freight trains carry huge loads.

They can have over

two hundred cars!

They can be two miles long!

Long trains need

more than one engine

to pull them.

Trains are great for hauling things.

They use less fuel than trucks.

They create less pollution.

Trains crisscross
the United States all day long.
They haul almost half its cargo.
They even carry trucks
filled with freight!

A truck reaches its stop.
Then it drives off
and delivers its goods.

Freight trains stop in rail yards
along their route.
They pick up new cars.
They leave other ones behind.
Some cars get unloaded there.
Some cars link with new trains
to get to their last stop.

Freight is often carried

in big boxes called containers.

They are lifted onto flatcars.

Flatcars carry lots of cargo.

They haul anything

that can get wet

if it rains or snows.

Even tanks can hitch a ride!

Cars are built
to carry different cargo.
Hopper cars are open
and easy to unload.
They work well for coal or sand.

Tankers hold liquids.

Some keep their cargo cold.

This tanker is full of juice!

Boxcars are closed,
so they keep cargo
clean and dry.
You never know
what could be inside!

# Trains in the City

Commuter trains take people

to the city each morning.

They bring them home at night.

Double-deckers

carry lots of passengers.

They save lots of gas too!

Train stations

can be a city's hub.

Commuter trains pull in.

Some trains depart

for faraway places.

Others arrive all day and night.

Travelers hop on trains
that take them around the city.
Subways are trains
that travel underground.
Subways use electricity to run.
A rail next to the tracks
supplies this power.

Subways can get very crowded.

In Japan,

men called pushers

help pack people in.

Trolleys travel on city streets.

They use electricity too.

It comes from wires above them

or underground.

Look up!

A train could be overhead.

Monorails do not use tracks.

They run on just one rail.

Rubber tires supply a quiet ride.

And you get a great view!

Want another great view?

Ride a funicular railway.

It goes up and down steep hills.

A funicular has two tracks.

It has one car on each of them.

They are joined by a cable.

The cable pulls one car uphill

as it pulls the other down.

# Fast and Faster

Long ago

trains used to be

the fastest way to travel.

Now we have jets.

But trains are moving faster too.

Old tracks slow trains down.

Some old tracks have curves.

Trains must brake

when going around a curve.

Some new trains

still use these tracks.

They just tilt while turning.

They lean the way bicycles do.

These trains go up to

150 miles an hour.

Most people in the United States
fly or drive between cities.
In other nations
people use trains instead.
New tracks have been laid.
The rails are straight.
So their trains go much faster.

Pointed high-speed trains

are called bullet trains.

Are they as fast as bullets?

Not really.

But they seem to fly!

Some go up to 220 miles an hour.

TGV trains in France go fast too.
One of them
was the world's fastest train.
It went 357 miles an hour!

Maglev trains do not have wheels.

Their tracks are different too.

Magnets make the trains float

above the rails.

Trains gliding on air go fast!

How fast?

One maglev races

360 miles an hour!

What else will new trains do?

Some new trains will weigh less.

A lighter train can save fuel.

Using less fuel means less pollution.

Some trains may have solar panels.

The sun's energy will help them run.

New trains will be
different inside too.
Look at this one!
Big glass windows.
Seats with movies and games.
Private compartments.
What a ride!

The trains of the future
will be amazing!

**Trains!**